Maurice Lemoine
on
Nicaragua

Leftwing or Fundamentalist?

Ovide Bastien

Published by Ovide Bastien

ISBN: 978-2-925157-25-0

Thanks to George Turski for kindly
proofreading this book

Other Books by Author

Chili: le coup divin published by "Les Éditions du Jour" in September 1974, in Montreal, Canada. Republished on Amazon as an eBook in 2014 and in paperback in 2015.

Chile: el golpe divino, published on Amazon as an eBook and in paperback in 2017. It includes a new section, Epíloga 2017.

Chile: The Divine Coup published on Amazon as an eBook and in paperback in 2017. It also includes a new section, Epilogue 2017.

CHILE: Underside of Economic Miracle published as a class manual at Dawson College from 1995 to 2011. Updated and republished on Amazon as an eBook in 2014 and in paperback in 2015.

My 9/11 Awakening to America's Moral Crisis (Diary and Letters, Chile: 11 September 1973 Military Coup), published on Amazon as an eBook and in paperback in 2015.

Love or Money: What Makes the World Go Round? published on Amazon as an eBook and in paperback in 2015.

Cry of the Earth – Cry of the Poor, published on Amazon as an eBook and in paperback in 2015.

Globalization Under Attack, published on Amazon as an eBook and in paperback in 2017.

Life of the Mind According to Aimé Forest, published on Amazon as an eBook and in paperback in 2018.

La vie de l'esprit selon Aimé Forest, published on Amazon as an eBook and in paperback in 2018.

Carl R. Rogers' Crisis: Subjectivity vs. Objectivity, published on Amazon as an eBook and in paperback in 2018.

La crise de Carl Rogers: Subjectivité vs objectivité, published on Amazon as an eBook and in paperback in 2018.

History of Zelaya Blandón Family, published on Amazon as an eBook and in paperback in 2018.

Historia de la Familia Zelaya Blandón, published on Amazon as an eBook and in paperback in 2018.

Roots of Crisis: Nicaragua 2018, published on Amazon as an eBook and in paperback in 2018.

Raíces de la crisis: Nicaragua 2018, published on Amazon as an eBook and in paperback in 2018.

Racines de la crise: Nicaragua 2018, published on Amazon as an eBook and in paperback in 2018.

Nicaragua selon Maurice Lemoine: gauche ou fondamentalisme?, published on Amazon as an eBook and in paperback in 2019.

¿Izquierda o fundamentalismo? Nicaragua según Maurice Lemoine, published on Amazon as an eBook and in paperback in 2019.

Conferences and Interviews

To see the talk I gave on Chile during the Social Forum in Ottawa on 22 August 2014:

https://www.youtube.com/watch?v=LJqi5bSLN0c

Christ Dayo from the CHRY News Collective interviewed me in late September 2014. To listen to this half-hour radio interview on the Chilean Coup:

https://www.mixcloud.com/discover/ovide-bastien/

To see my 5-minute 2014 homage (mostly in French) to Sister Marie Denise Dubois, a woman who dedicated her life to the marginalized in Chile and Honduras:

Marie Denise Dubois ou l'autre visage de l'Église

To see the talk I gave on Chile – I was invited by the Egyptian Canadian Coalition for Democracy – during the World Social Forum in Montreal on 10 August 2016, go here (The talk is in French) : Ovide Bastien| L'Égypte entre démocratie et dictature

For more information about the author: (https://www.amazon.com/kindle-dbs/author/ref=dbs_a_mng_awm_scns_share%3F_encoding=UTF8&asin=B015UHPY80)

Table of Contents

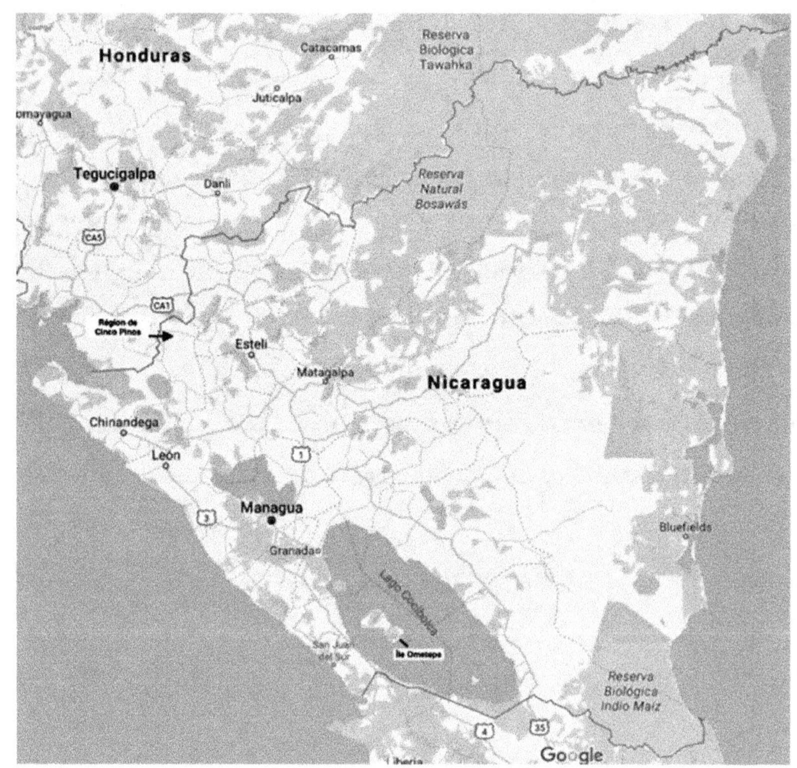

Honduras
Catacamas
Reserva
Biológica
Tawahka
Juticalpa
omayagua
Tegucigalpa
Danli
Reserva
Natural
Bosawás
CA5
CA1
Región de
Cinco Pinos
Esteli
Matagalpa
Nicaragua
Chinandega
León
1
Managua
Bluefields
3
Granada
Lago Cocibolca
Isla Ometepe
San Juan
del Sur
Reserva
Biológica
Indio Maíz
4
35
Liberia
Google

Nicaragua

Contempt for the suffering of Nicaraguans

As notes the former editor-in-chief of *Le Monde Diplomatique*, Maurice Lemoine, in his January 18, 2019 article <u>Quand on veut noyer l'ALBA, on l'accuse d'avoir la rage</u> (When one wants to get rid of ALBA, one accuses it of having rabies)[1], it is obvious that we are currently witnessing a comeback of the right in Latin America and that the United States is seeking to support and exploit this situation. This is reflected, he says, in the words of US National Security Advisor John Bolton who, in November 2018, referred to Cuba, Nicaragua and Venezuela - all members of the Bolivarian Alliance for the Peoples of Our America (ALBA) - as a "troika of tyranny" and a "triangle of terror".

However, I find Lemoine's analysis very troubling. In essence, and starting from his global observation (about the right), he views very positively the behavior of the Ortega-Murillo government in Nicaragua while taking a very critical stand regarding the hundreds of thousands of protesters demanding the departure of the Ortega-Murillo couple. Even if he demonstrates a remarkable knowledge of the current situation in Latin America, I believe that Lemoine, in his analysis of Nicaragua, shows a fundamentalism that is very similar to that found so often in the realm of religion.

---

[1] *Mémoire de luttes* (Memory of Struggles). Accessed on January 19, 2019.

Readers who know little about the history of Nicaragua, except perhaps for the main features of the extraordinary Sandinista revolution of the 80s, the rise of the neoliberal right from 1990 to 2006, and the return, in 2007, of an FSLN that adopts the slogan "solidarity, socialist, and Christian" accompanied by John Lennon's song Peace and Love, will undoubtedly be very impressed by the numerous facts presented by Lemoine to support his thesis according to which what happened in Nicaragua represents another coup attempt, financed and supported by the American empire and the Nicaraguan right. An attempt cleverly disguised as a sudden, massive, and peaceful popular uprising, but which, according to Lemoine, was not at all spontaneous and popular, and even less peaceful.

What troubles me in the analysis presented by Lemoine are not the facts and events he reports, but rather those he omits. And above all, the fact that he turns a blind eye - a dismissiveness tantamount to a form of contempt - towards the immense suffering of Nicaraguans, the majority of whom are currently plunged into mourning, suffering, economic insecurity and fear.

I consider myself left-wing, but I want to dissociate myself completely from the type of left that Maurice Lemoine seems to embody. And in what follows, I will try to explain why.

I want to make it clear that even though Lemoine's analysis not only deals with the situation in Nicaragua - he refers to the current crisis in Venezuela, discusses the global situation in Latin America, and even the "gilets jaunes" demonstrations in France - I will limit my comments to his observations about the situation in Nicaragua, a country I have been visiting annually for the last 23 years - from 1995 to 2011 accompanying students of the Dawson College North South Studies program, and from 2012 to 2018 managing, on a volunteer basis, development projects - and of which I have a deeper knowledge.

The basis tension: can the left be critical without falling into betrayal?

Underlying my criticism of Maurice Lemoine's analysis of the present Nicaraguan crisis, one finds a basic issue facing today's entire political left: up to what extent can one be critical of a progressive (or even revolutionary) government without in so doing promoting the agenda of right-wing forces and/or American imperialism?

In any conflict, it is obvious that any position, criticism or analysis can (and will) be used by one or other of the opponents if they think this can support their cause. So how can one manage to remain critical and avoid becoming subservient, in a servile and obligatory manner, to a government that claims to be progressive, left-wing, revolutionary or Bolivarian? How can one avoid becoming the cheerleader or unconditional defender of a government one has supported in the past, but which, though claiming to be doing things "in the name of the people", is governing in an ever more dictatorial manner?

Zimbabwe's Robert Mugabe is a good example to illustrate what I mean. A military leader of the Zimbabwe African National Union (ZANU), one of the two armed liberation movements fighting against the colonial authorities of Southern Rhodesia, he was elected prime minister in internationally supervised democratic elections in March 1980. In 1987, he became president of Zimbabwe by transforming the country into a one-party presidential regime and started governing in an increasingly authoritarian (if not dictatorial) manner until the venerable age of 93. In 2017, to avoid being legally removed, he was finally forced to resign. This revolutionary political leader held power without interruption and in a fairly absolute manner for thirty-seven years. By the end of his reign, he had become a pathetic caricature of himself and was carrying on as a full-fledged dictator ready to do anything to hold on to power, and eventually bequeath it to his second wife. When did it become legitimate (or even necessary) to criticize a government that had started out as being authentically revolutionary? Up to what extent and for how long can someone, who claims to be left-wing, continue supporting a ruler who says he prioritizes the common good of his nation, but imposes his agenda by force and increasingly clings to power by mere repression?

Such challenging questions seem to apply to Nicaragua, a country with whose people I have developed very deep bonds over the last decades. I was an active supporter of the Sandinista revolution in the 1980s and presently have close friends on both sides of the political divide.

Given that my Nicaraguan partners for most of the student field trips that I have organized in the last twenty three years and development projects in which I have participated were not only supporters of the FSLN, but also, as they say in Nicaragua, Orteguistas, that is admirers of Daniel Ortega, raising these questions has proven to be a very taxing and heart wrenching experience for me.

.

Lemoine's views and my critique

First, I will reproduce Lemoine's views regarding the Nicaraguan crisis. Then, I will critically examine these views.

My critique will be based on the criterion that Lemoine himself considers fundamental for all qualitative journalistic reporting. A reporter, he insists, should always seek to report events with nuance and precision, situating them carefully in their appropriate context and scrupulously avoiding retaining only those which reflect his dogmas and beliefs. And that is precisely, according to him, what mainstream media no longer does.

> "Most of mainstream media has long forgotten the meaning of the word contextualize," asserts Lemoine. This is particularly true of the mainstream media coverage of the Nicaraguan crisis, which "did not go out of its way to seek nuance or precision, most mainstream media outlets having taken the fatal habit of ignoring that part reality that does not reflect their dogmas and beliefs."

One can hardly find fault with Lemoine's criterion of what should characterize all rigorous and intellectually honest journalistic reporting. But let's see how he himself lives up to this criterion in his media coverage of the Nicaraguan crisis.

Number of victims

When I listened on YouTube to the December 20, 2018 report presented in Washington by the Interdisciplinary Group of Independent Experts (IEG) of the Organization of American States (OAS), at one point I broke down in tears. These may have resulted from some of the pain I still felt after the recent replacement of my two knees. But I think my tears came mainly from the immense sadness I felt because of the suffering of the Nicaraguan people, well described in the report. And also, the testimony of a Nicaraguan friend who, upon recently arriving in Montreal after spending two months with her peasant family in Nicaragua, told me:

> "Ovide, no one in my family and my region is talking about what's happening in Nicaragua. People are living in fear."

A few days later when I tried, during a telephone conversation, to explain to a close left-wing friend whose lifelong generosity for the marginalized is absolutely remarkable, what I had felt while listening to the report of the GIEI, he immediately interrupted me:

> "Ovide, stop, stop... I do not want to know anything about this group of experts who work for the OAS. This organization is right-wing, and I have no confidence whatsoever in its report; I simply will not read it!"

Taken aback, I just changed the subject. I was a bit hurt emotionally as I had not even been able to tell him that I had broken down in tears as I read the report.

When I was young, my rural and very Catholic family strongly believed no one in our family should ever marry a Protestant, or someone from a religion other than Catholicism. The human qualities of a non-Catholic person, however extraordinary they may be, mattered little. What mattered the most was marrying a person who adhered to our faith.

****

Like my left-wing friend, Lemoine does not seem to trust the GIEI report. Nor the other numerous reports that basically say the same things: the report prepared by the United Nations High Commissioner "Violations of Human Rights and Abuses in the Context of the Protests in Nicaragua: April 18th to 18th August 2018;" or those prepared by the Inter-American Commission on Human Rights (IACHR), the Nicaraguan Center for Human Rights, and Amnesty International.

In his criticism of the GIEI report, Lemoine calls into question the scientific value and impartiality of the inquiry on which it relies. This report "on the violence committed between April 18 and May 30" is of a very doubtful scientific rigor, he says, because its officials admit themselves that their investigation is based only on the interview "of families of victims, 'survivors of repression', refugees, (...) press articles (opposition media!) and a 'rigorous' analysis of photographs, more than three million Tweets and ten thousand videos posted by opponents on social networks."

Lemoine calls into question the number of victims reported by the GIEI. It has been shown, he says, that "opposition and local human rights NGOs have added to the list of victims 253 people who have been victims of villainous homicide, common crimes, traffic accidents, suicides, etc., this in order to manipulate national and international opinion through the mainstream media."

The number of victims reported by the GIEI, the United Nations High Commissioner and human rights NGOs is of little importance to Lemoine; his faith (his politico-ideological credo) is elsewhere. He believes in the Ortega government. He believes the Ortega government report that the crisis would have caused only 197 deaths, and that the opposition, Nicaraguan NGOs, and international organizations intentionally inflated this figure in order to denigrate the Ortega government.

But what small detail, which could add nuance, quality and precision to Lemoine's analysis and demonstrate that he has not forgotten the meaning of the word "contextualize", does he fail to mention because it does not reflect his dogmas and beliefs?

The very important and telling fact that when the GIEI, the Nicaraguan human rights organizations and the United Nations High Commissioner repeatedly asked the Ortega government, during the ongoing crisis, to provide them with the information it had about the number of deaths, injuries and missing persons, the names of the deceased and the circumstances surrounding their deaths, so that they could compare and, if necessary, correct their own data, the government always flatly refused, only accepting to release the names of the 22 victims of the police forces.

> "The only dead whose identities it has publicly revealed are 21 policemen", comments Chamorro. Why the silence and secrecy regarding the other 301 deaths? And why would the Ortega government, on the one hand refuse to cooperate with the IACHR, not providing them with their list of deaths so that a comparison can be made between the government list and that of the IACHR, and, on the other hand, accuse the IACHR of producing a biased report, which conflates the deaths related to the civic protest with those resulting from common crimes?"[2]

---

[2] Carlos Chamorro, "Los "falsos positivos" de la matanza de Ortega" (False Positives of the Ortega Slaughter), *Confidencial*, August 20, 2018. Accessed the same day.

Unfortunately, notes the GIEI in the introduction of its report, our investigation was weakened because of the lack of collaboration of the "organs of the State of Nicaragua, which did not provide the requested documents, nor did they respond to our requests to meet with them". That is why we had to limit ourselves, with regret, to the interview of the family of victims, the analysis of articles of press, etc.

But Lemoine, instead of reporting this flagrant lack of collaboration from the Ortega government, which questions its credibility, does exactly the opposite. He blames the GIEI and accuses it of lacking scientific rigor and impartiality, precisely because its investigation was based only on the interview of "families of victims, 'survivors of repression', refugees, (...) press articles (opposition media!) and a rigorous analysis of the photographs, more than three million Tweets and ten thousand videos posted by the opponents on the social networks."

One would expect much more, in terms of journalistic quality, from the former chief editor of such a prestigious newspaper as *Le Monde Diplomatique*! Lemoine reports as weakness, as lack of scientific rigor and impartiality the fact that the investigators of the GIEI did not include the data of the government in their report, though it is the government itself that systematically refused to provide such data! He thus demonstrates, and in a very blatant manner, the same lack of rigor and intellectual honesty that he attributes to mainstream media: reporting with scant precision and nuance, forgetting the meaning of the word "contextualize" and, above all, ignoring those parts of reality that do not fit his dogmas and beliefs.

Pro-Ortega paramilitaries

Lemoine affirms that "there was no intervention of paramilitaries" in Nicaragua, but rather, "in the great Nicaraguan tradition, the outburst of 'civil war' involving murderous excesses on both sides". After mentioning the student demonstrations of April 2018 against the reform of the Nicaraguan Institute of Social Security (INSS), a reform quickly abandoned by Ortega in an attempt to calm things, he describes in the following terms the beginning of what he sees as the outburst of civil war:

> "It is the Business Association of Nicaragua (Cosep), concealed behind the facade of the "autoconvocados" (self-organized) students, more likely to provoke sympathy, and a very motley Civic Alliance, composed of sectors each with of its own political agenda, that suddenly started calling for 'the departure of Ortega'- forgetting the INSS. And then, on the ground, the situation degenerated. Firearms and homemade mortars, arson, barricades ("tranques"), looting, destruction of official and private buildings: an insurrectional violence, that had nothing to do with students, that was not at all "peaceful" and 'spontaneous', and which caused as many civil and police victims as the repression with which it was met. The events did not move media watchdogs; any voice departing from the 'official' story was automatically eliminated."

That the vast majority of observers, both Nicaraguan and international, recognize that the key element that triggered the massive popular uprising against the Ortega government was the brutal and lethal violence of the pro-Ortega paramilitaries against students, matters little to Lemoine. Not only does he not recognize the existence of such violence by pro-Ortega paramilitaries, but he even denies the very existence of these paramilitaries!

Instead, he points to "insurrectional violence" as the main cause of what he describes as a traditional "civil war". According to Lemoine, the student protesters merely represent a façade - students being "more likely to provoke sympathy" - to conceal an attempt to overthrow the Ortega government: nothing more. And the demand, coming from hundreds of thousands of demonstrators for the departure of the Ortega-Murillo couple, only reflects a plot - at once an integral part of the comeback of the right in Latin America - to overthrow the government.

That as early as May 21, 2014[3] the bishops of the Nicaraguan Catholic Church were already accusing the Ortega government of the fact that its police were standing idly by when pro-government paramilitary groups violently attacked peaceful protesters, information that could help one contextualize the April 2018 crisis and help one better understand its deep roots, does not matter to Lemoine. His faith is in Daniel Ortega.

That Nicaraguan NGOs, the IACHR, Amnesty International, and the GIEI all acknowledge and deplore the existence of pro-Ortega paramilitaries, this hardly impresses Lemoine.

That the United Nations High Commissioner affirms, in his report of 29 August 2018, that "information obtained by the OHCHR clearly indicates that pro-government Ortega armed elements, including those known as 'shock forces', or 'hordes', have acted, often jointly and in coordination with the national police, and with the approval of many state authorities (...) and have participated in raids and attacks on protesters and

---

[3] "En búsqueda de nuevos horizontes para una nicaragua mejor". See paragraph 18 of the Bishops' statement. Accessed August 15, 2018.

carried out unlawful detentions," that does not impress Lemoine either.

And that even Daniel Ortega's own brother, Humberto, who led the Sandinista revolutionary army during all the years of the revolution and in the early years of Violeta Chamorro's government, recognizes and deplores the existence of these paramilitaries,[4] that does not impress Lemoine any more. No. His faith is elsewhere. He believes the narrative of Daniel Ortega who, in the many interviews he gave to Fox News, CNN, Telesur, Euronews, etc. during the weeks following the outbreak of the crisis, maintained that such paramilitaries simply did not exist.

That the GIEI, the United Nations High Commissioner, the IACHR, as well as all the Nicaraguan and international NGOs clearly state that most of the victims are on the side of the demonstrators, that is of little importance for Lemoine. His faith is elsewhere. He believes the Ortega government's claim that there were as many casualties on one side as the other. Lemoine knows, in his deeply revolutionary leftist faith, who is right. He knows that the right systematically distorts reality and that the truth lies with Ortega. He endorses the Ortega government's assertion that "the IACHR manipulates the information, presenting a coup attempt as a mere peaceful demonstration, and deliberately omitting to mention that the murdered persons are mainly police officers, State workers, Sandinista militants and civilians not involved in the conflict."[5]

---

[4] "El mundo ya sabe lo que pasa en Nicaragua" (The World Now Knows What's Happening in Nicaragua), *Envío*, August 2018. Accessed September 1, 2018.
[5] Yader Luna, Gobierno de Ortega ataca a la CIDH, (Ortega Government Attacks IACHR Report), *Confidencial*, August 19, 2018. Accessed August 21, 2018.

Money from Washington to prepare and finance the overthrow of Ortega

Lemoine also reports the sums of money received from Washington by the independent media and civil society in Nicaragua, making it clear that this money had nothing to do with social justice and peace and was aimed squarely at overthrowing Ortega.

> "Over the 2010-2020 period, USAID - i.e. Washington - has budgeted more than $ 68 million to its Nicaraguan 'friends' - over and above the $7,995,022 allocated in 2016 for a 'media-building program,' says Lemoine. To implement this, the Violeta Barrios de Chamorro Foundation (named after the rightist ex-president) alone received $2,530,000. For its part, the NED was also very generous with its main 'clients' Hagamos Democracia (Let's Create Democracy) ($ 525,000 since 2014) and IEEPP ($260,000 over the same period)."

However, Lemoine ignores the amount of money received in recent years from Venezuela - about $ 500 million a year until recently - by Daniel Ortega. This massive aid, in the form of oil sold on favorable terms, was not directed to the Government of Nicaragua as such. It was privatized, going directly to the FSLN, a political party which, following the defeat of the Sandinistas in 1989, had gradually wiped out its revolutionary program, becoming more and more an instrument of the Ortega family dynasty.[6] While 40% of Venezuelan aid financed laudable social programs while fortifying the political support of the government in rural

---

[6] See Dora María Téllez, "El Frente Sandinista colapsó, ahora es la maquinaria política de una familia" (The FSLN Collapsed: It's Now the Plitical Machine of a Family), *Envío*, January 2013. Accessed August 15, 2018.

areas, the other 60% was used to enrich the Ortega couple, which became, with their many children and their spouses, owners of large businesses, including the property of most of Nicaragua's media.[7]

Lemoine also fails to mention the fact that until recently the Nicaraguan private sector (Cosep) was a very close ally of the Ortega government. That such a close ally would, suddenly and out of the blue, decide to join a motley Civic Alliance to overthrow the government seems surprising.

Also overlooked is the fact that Ortega has been working closely with the IMF in recent years and has always welcomed with open arms American, European, Canadian, and other investments.

One wonders whether the foregoing information, omitted from Lemoine's media coverage of Nicaragua, would allow readers to add nuance and precision and help contextualize things. Did the assistance received from Washington by the independent media and civil society, quite modest compared to Venezuelan aid, really originate, as Lemoine suggests, from the great concern on the part of the Nicaraguan private sector and the United States about a "socialist and revolutionary" government that had to be overthrown in order not to harm national capitalist interests and American investments?

Why should one attempt to smash open a door that is already wide open? Why should one attack an economic model that, though proclaiming itself to be socialist, basically reproduces the main characteristics of neoliberalism, including the enrichment of the ruling elite?

---

[7] David Adams et Wilfredo Miranda Aburto, Daniel Inc: How Nicaragua's Ortega financed a political dynasty, Univision News, May 5, 2018. Accessed September 7, 2018. See also Carlos Chamorro and Carlos Maldonado, "Las cuentas secretas de Albanisa," (Secret Accounts of Albanisa), *Confidencial*, March 5, 2011. Accessed September 7, 2018.

The Catholic Church supports the coup attempt?

As Ollantay Itzamna did in his blog on Telesur on July 11, 2018,[8] Lemoine attacks the role played by the leaders of the Catholic Church during the Nicaraguan crisis. Clearly suggesting, as Daniel Ortega himself has done many times, that the Catholic Church has supported a coup attempt, he scathingly criticizes its leaders, quoting Jesus according to the Gospel of St. Matthew:

> "Woe to you, teachers of the law and Pharisees, you hypocrites! You are like whitewashed tombs, which look beautiful on the outside but on the inside are full of the bones of the dead and everything unclean. In the same way, on the outside you appear to people as righteous but, on the inside, you are full of hypocrisy and wickedness!"

In order to demonstrate "the direct links of the ecclesiastical hierarchy with the bloody attempt of destabilization", Lemoine refers to the audio recording of a private conversation of the auxiliary bishop of the Archdiocese of Managua, Mgr. Silvio Báez, with peasant leaders, recorded without the bishop's knowledge and "made public by the Christian community St. Paul the Apostle, of the colony September 14 (in the east of Managua)": Audio conspirativo del obispo Silvio Baez, presentado esta mañana por la Comunidad Cristiana (Conspiracy audio recording of Bishop Báez presented this morning by the Christian Community).

What information, which could help readers understand in its appropriate context the role played by the leaders of the Catholic Church during the crisis, is omitted by Lemoine?

---

[8] "¿Guerra santa en Nicaragua?." (Holy War in Nicaragua?). Accessed August 20, 2018.

What reality does he ignore, possibly because it does not reflect his dogmas and beliefs?

During the National Dialogue between protesters and the government, which began in May 2018, the Bishop of Estelí, Mgr. Abelardo Mata, made a very emotional appeal:

> "Mr. President, (…) an unarmed revolution is under way in Nicaragua. (…) Here, one does not find an army confronting an army. One finds instead a nation expressing everything that it has been feeling for several years, complaints that we had the opportunity to express to the government on May 21, 2014.[9] Do you want to dismantle the revolution through repression, with rubber bullets, lead bullets, and paramilitary forces?"[10]

Above, I mentioned one of the grievances of the Nicaraguan population to which Bishop Mata refers, and that the bishops had presented to the Ortega government in May 2014: the fact that the national police often remained idle, while pro-Ortega paramilitaries violently attacked peaceful protesters. Let's take a look at some of the other grievances, which obviously shed light on the deep roots of the April 2018 uprising.

The Nicaraguan bishops criticize the "cruel and degrading inhuman treatment" to which prisoners - both national and foreign citizens - are subjected, especially in El Chipote prisons whose closure they also demand.

____

[9] Nicaraguan bishops met with Daniel Ortega on May 21, 2014. They then produced a document, "En búsqueda de nuevos horizontes para una Nicaragua mejor" (Searching for New horizons for a Better Nicaragua), which presents to the public what they told him. Accessed August 2, 2018.

[10] "Así habló en el diálogo Juan Abelardo Mata, obispo de Estelí," (How Bishop of Estelí, Mons. Juan Abelardo Mata, Spoke During National Dialogue), posted on YouTube May 16, 2018. Accessed August 9, 2018.

They argue that the government's employment policy only favors government supporters, and that state employees, whether Sandinista or not, sometimes see part of their salary deducted in support of the FSLN.

They claim that state employees must also, regardless of their political affiliation, participate in partisan activities of the FSLN, otherwise they risk losing their jobs.

They highlight the complaints they regularly receive from indigenous populations living near nature reserves, such as Indio Maíz, exploited by companies and individuals close to the government, and this in a predatory manner and in total disregard of environmental laws and "under the protection of corrupt municipal and national authorities".

In a clear reference to the Ortega family's almost monopolistic hold on the media, they criticize "the growing monopolization of the media".

Without explicitly mentioning Rosario Murillo's daily televised messages to the public in the state media, they criticize the use of religious signs and values in slogans and state propaganda in which "the ruling party is identified to God's Divine Providence" and its ideology presented as if it were a 'cult to God'.

Finally, the bishops denounce, "as of the outcome of the 2011 elections, the concentration of power, government corruption, the attempt to identify the ruling party with the state, the subjection of the powers of the State to the will of the Executive, the disrespect for the laws, the lack of legal security, influence peddling, political intolerance, domination by the executive of most of the mayors of the country (...)." [11]

---

[11] The information in these latter paragraphs was drawn from, "En búsqueda de nuevos horizontes para una Nicaragua mejor", to which we referred to above.

When the pensioners, in 2013, had demonstrated massively against the Ortega government, they had suffered, and this in the presence of a complicit police, a brutal repression on the part of the Sandinista Youth July 19, hooded and carrying firearms. The auxiliary bishop of Managua, Mgr. Silvio José Báez, immediately denounced this repression, describing the government operation as 'state terrorism'.[12]

Luciana Chamorro and Emilia Yang, who claim that this 'state terrorism' of 2013 was a precursor of the 'state terrorism' of April 2018, describe this event in the following manner :

> "At dawn on June 22, 2013 at 4 o'clock in the morning, the camp of protestors is attacked. Approximately 300 hooded armed civilians linked to the Sandinista Youth July 19 (JS) arrive at the site in four trucks, property of the Mayor of Managua. They assault more than 50 youth and 35 retirees, spraying gasoline on them, threatening them with death and rape, stripping and assaulting them with sticks, hammers, machetes and firearms. In addition, they steal about $ 80,000 of their personal belongings, including seven cars and donations they had received in support of the protest. Cars passing by the scene notify state firemen, but the latter refuse to come and help the protestors who are victims of aggression. And all this happens in the presence of at least 30 members of the National Police who are present, guarding the INSS building.

---

[12] "#OcupaInss, un precedente de Terrorismo de Estado," (#OcupaInss: Precursor of State Terrorism), *Confidencial*, June 22, 2018. Accessed August 5, 2018.

> "The use of state resources and institutions makes it ultra-clear that the whole operation is planned by the top leaders of the Ortega regime."[13]

Just as Bishop Báez had played a leadership role in the Ortega government's denouncement of state terrorism against pensioners and the students who supported them in 2013, he played an even more prominent leadership role in denouncing the state terrorism practiced by Ortega in April 2018.

> "His popularity was growing until, in the last demonstrations, he appeared as its main leader in encouraging his countrymen to speak out freely, comments José Manuel Vidal. He also shows leadership in requesting that they abstain, even after the bloodshed of young and innocent students whose only crime was to demand democracy and freedom, from falling into the perverse dynamics of violence and death of the Ortega regime. (…)

> "President Ortega is aware of Báez' leadership and keeps an eye on him. The bishop is underdoing attacks from the government that are orchestrated by pro-government journalists, official media and anonymous accounts on social networks, such as Facebook and Twitter, where Mgr. Baez has been very active for years. (...)

> "The Ortega government repeats and copies against Bishop Báez the same techniques the Salvadoran extreme right used against the soon-to-be new saint, Mgr. Romero, which ended in his assassination. They accuse Bishop Báez of being

---

[13] "#OcupaInss, un precedente de Terrorismo de Estado," *Confidencial*, June 22, 2018. Accessed August 5, 2018.

'the head of subversion', and because of this he has received several death threats."[14]

If Lemoine had taken the trouble to learn more about the concrete situation in Nicaragua, instead of seeing everything through the prism - comeback of the right in Latin America with the support of the United States - he would have recognized that the leaders of the Catholic Church in Nicaragua played a prophetic and courageous role during the April 2018 crisis, showing great compassion for the people and their demands. And that it is because of this compassion and solidarity that they enjoy a very high credibility with the population, unlike that of the Ortega government, which, like the economy, is in a downward spiral.

And if he had taken the trouble to learn more about the recent history of Nicaragua, he would have learned that Daniel Ortega has systematically been using, and this for a long time, smear campaigns to crush all those who denounce his faults and oppose him. Here is an example, among many others.

In 1998, at the age of 30, Zoilamérica, daughter of Rosario Murillo, astonishes Nicaragua: she declares that Daniel Ortega has sexually abused her since the age of 11 and publishes a 48-page document containing the details of these abuses.

Shortly afterwards, another shocking news hits the nation: ex-right-wing President Arnoldo Alemán is accused of pocketing a substantial portion of Nicaragua's international aid following Hurricane Mitch.

In the months that follow, Ortega manages to conclude with his former political arch enemy, Alemán, a pact which, by

---

[14] José Manuel Vidal, "Silvio Báez, el obispo que hizo frente al 'comandante' Ortega," (Silvio Báez, Bishop who Confronted Ortega), *Religión Digital*, May 5, 2018. Accessed May 20, 2018.

assuring them both a seat in the National Assembly for the next two terms, confers on them years of parliamentary immunity. Alemán thus escapes 20 years of prison, and Ortega is protected from judicial pursuits from Zoilamérica.

When the women's movement, whose autonomy in Nicaragua is particularly strong, repeatedly and publicly denounces, under the leadership of Sofia Montenegro, the Ortega-Alemán Pact and the ensuing impunity obtained by Ortega in the Zoilamérica case, Ortega launches a smear campaign against Montenegro. For months, the website of President Ortega's office has on its home page the title 'An agent named Montenegro' whose hyperlink refers to an article in the personal magazine of Rosario Murillo, in which it is stated that Sofía Montenegro is a CIA agent.

The smear campaign deepens in October 2008, when a team of prosecutors, supported by 40 police officers, raid the office of the Communication Investigation Center (Cinco), headed by Sofia Montenegro and Carlos Fernando Chamorro, and seize the files, computers and books found there. The alleged purpose of the raid: the search for evidence relating to fraud and money laundering. The specific accusation against Cinco: allocating money to a group of women - those making life hard for Ortega about the Zoilamérica Affair - who have no legal status.[15]

Weakened by the great compassion and solidarity expressed by the leaders of the Catholic Church towards the population during the crisis of April 2018, and especially by the leadership of Bishop Báez, Ortega immediately has recourse to his old and well-known tactics of smear campaigns. Accused of being responsible for the death of hundreds and

---

[15] Claudia Korol, "No a la injerencia extranjera. Solo el pueblo salva al pueblo "(No to Foreign Intervention. Only the People Saves the People), *Marcha*, December 26, 2018. Accessed on the same day. Also see Tina Rosenberg, "The Many Stories of Carlos Fernando Chamorro," *The New York Times Magazine,* March 20, 2009. Accessed August 20, 2018.

the wounds of thousands of Nicaraguans, Ortega hits back by accusing the Catholic Church of being responsible for these tragic events by being complicit in the massive demonstrations he describes as "a bloody coup attempt". Part of this well-orchestrated governmental smear campaign is the release, on state media, of the recording of Mgr. Báez's private conversation with peasants.

The day after the publication of the audio recording of Mgr. Báez to which Lemoine refers, *Channel 4*, property of the Ortega family, makes a 17-minute long report titled "Silvio Báez and his criminal and conspiratorial coup plan against the people of Nicaragua" (Silvio Báez en planes golpistas, criminales y conspirativos contra el pueblo de Nicaragua). The report begins with the following words:

> "Silvio Báez confirmed his active participation in terrorist activities and the coup against the people of Nicaragua. Pro-abortionists and drug traffickers are some of those he recruited to achieve his goal. The Christian Community Saint Paul the Apostle released the audio recording[16] in which Silvio Báez confessed his crimes."

Lemoine fails to mention the fact that Bishop Báez claims that the audio recording was manipulated, and that following its publication he was the object of "many threats, even death threats, and that paramilitaries were going around his house on motorbikes at night."[17] Instead, he compares Bishop Báez and the leaders of the Nicaraguan Catholic Church to those

---

[16] Here is the hyperlink for this audio recording: Audio conspirativo del obispo Silvio Baez, presentado esta mañana por la Comunidad Cristiana. (Conspirator Audio of Bishop Báez, Published this Morning by Christian Community). Accessed October 25, 2018.

[17] Monseñor Silvio Báez dice que audio que lo señala como terrorista es manipulado (Bishop Silvio Báez Says Audio that Claims he is a Terrorist Was Altered), video posted on *Canal 10* October 25, 2018. Accessed November 8, 2018.

"scribes and Pharisees" denounced by Jesus as hypocrites, who "look beautiful on the outside but on the inside are full of the bones of the dead and everything unclean."

A deeper knowledge of Nicaragua would have enabled Lemoine to understand that this quote from Jesus fits rather well the behavior of the Ortega-Murillo couple since the outbreak of the crisis, and in particular that of Rosario Murillo, who, in her daily televised speeches to the nation, reflects a religious fanaticism where Christian love for one's neighbor goes hand in hand with the systematic denigration of the demonstrators, portrayed as coup plotters, terrorists, and satanical forces of evil.

Repression of independent media

Lemoine mentions the raid carried out by the police on December 14, 2018 of the "premises of the online media *Confidencial*, which is directed by Carlos Fernando Chamorro, the son of the former president," but he does so without showing any indignation regarding such blatant repression of the media. On the contrary, he seems to consider this raid quite normal and simply describes Carlos as "the main spokesperson of the right", an independent journalist who "has benefited from the disinterested generosity of the NED for years, is the 'modest' owner of *La Prensa, Hoy, Confidencial, Esta Noche, Esta Semana* (companies where unions have never been authorized) -, the Communication Investigation Center (Cinco) and the Violeta Barrios de Chamorro Foundation."

Lemoine also does not seem to be at all upset about another raid carried out by the police a few days later, this time against the offices of the television station *100% Noticias*. On the contrary, he seems to consider altogether normal the closing of this channel and the indictment and imprisonment of its owner, Miguel Mora, and his press director, Lucia

Pineda "for provocation, incitement and conspiracy to commit terrorist acts."

Let's see how Lemoine, here again, passes the test of the journalistic principle which is so dear to him - reporting with precision and nuance and situating events in their appropriate context.

Who exactly is Miguel Mora, this journalist imprisoned for 'conspiracy' and 'terrorism'?

For years, the Ortega regime considered *100% Noticias* as a quasi-governmental television channel, although it is private. Why? Because Miguel Mora, its director, was a party activist and promoted the FSLN agenda on his channel. Although *100% Noticias* offered, in its desire to live up to professional journalism, a diversified programming and occasionally presented criticisms which irritated the government, the Ortega-Murillo couple considered it one of its own. The dramatic changeover in *100% Noticias* programming took place "only at the beginning of the massive popular uprising of April 2018," comments Guillemo Cortés Dominguez. Specifically following "the assault of a team of its journalists and the theft of a television camera of great value," the order received from the government "to no longer report on the popular revolt," then, when he refused the order, the government censorship that struck him temporarily. It was then that Mora transformed the programming of *100% Noticias*, rendering it day by day ever more the voice of those who mobilized massively against the government.[18]

Lemoine fails to mention this 'contextual' information and he also ignores the fact, which would add enormously to the

---

[18] Guillemo Cortés Dominguez, "100 Noticias: una piedra en el zapato de la dictadura," (100 Noticias: A Pain in the Neck for Dictatorship), *Confidencial*, December 24, 2018. Accessed January 5, 2019.

quality and precision of his analysis, that Mora and Pineda, like the 600 or so other political prisoners, are currently facing bogus trials that in no way respect the most basic criteria of the rule of law.[19]

It can therefore be concluded that Lemoine does not pass the test of his own journalistic principle in the case of *100% Noticias*.

What about his claim that Carlos Fernando Chamorro is the "main spokesperson of the right" in Nicaragua, and that one should therefore not be very surprised at the government crackdown suffered by the media outlets that he owns?

Who is Carlos Chamorro?

Before answering this question, I would first like to point out that, contrary to what Lemoine asserts, Carlos Chamorro, to my knowledge, is in no way the owner of *La Prensa*, *Hoy*, and the Violeta Barrios de Chamorro Foundation.

I met Carlos in 1976 when I was studying for my master's degree in economics at McGill University and he was studying for a bachelor's degree in the same subject matter. At Christmas 1977, Carlos, son of Pedro Joaquín Chamorro

---

[19] In its report, the GIEI states, on page 230: "Hundreds of people who took part in the protest or who are considered to be opposition parties are currently undergoing criminal proceedings. According to the president of the Supreme Court of Justice, at the end of November, there were 546 people accused (...). According to the information available, (...) these criminal proceedings are vitiated by serious violations of the guarantees of due process, including arrests and searches without warrant outside the cases provided by law, failure to respect the 48 hours to the maximum laid down in the constitution to be presented to a judge, the automatic and unfounded use of preventive imprisonment, the formulation of indeterminate charges, ... an unreasonable assessment of the evidence, the omission of hypotheses favorable to the defense arising from the evidence presented, (...)."

and Violeta Chamorro, returned to Nicaragua for the mid-term leave. On January 10, 1978, his father, owner and editor of *La Prensa*, the most important newspaper of Nicaragua and also the most critical of the Somoza dictatorship, was assassinated by the dictator. This event triggered, during the historic funeral service, a massive protest against Somoza that considerably deepened and speeded up the armed uprising against Somoza. Carlos decided to leave his studies at McGill and stayed in his country to join the fight against Somoza until his historic overthrow on July 19, 1979.

The Sandinista government quickly founded a newspaper, *Barricada*, which became a principal organ speaking for the revolution, and it is Carlos who became its director, a position that he would occupy until the beginning of the nineties.

It was not until 1994 that Carlos was dismissed from his post as director of *Barricada*. The reason for his dismissal? Although the FSLN accepted, following its electoral defeat in 1990, that *Barricada* would cut off its close ties with the FSLN and start practicing professional journalism, Daniel Ortega changed his mind when he himself found himself increasingly the object of the paper's criticism. He summoned Carlos and demanded that *Barricada* stop criticizing him. When Carlos refused, Ortega fired him on the spot.[20]

The departure of Carlos caused a crisis in the newspaper as more than 80% of the journalists of *Barricada* resigned.

---

[20] It was during a conference given to the students of the Dawson College North-South Studies program in January 2006 that Carlos Chamorro explained the circumstances of his dismissal from *Barricada*. For more information see the book Beyond the Barricades, (Ohio University Press, 2002) in which Adam Jones relates the history of *Barricada*.

Reorganized under the leadership of Tomás Borge, *Barricada* went bankrupt four years later.

Carlos comes from a family whose members, though supportive of the struggle against Somoza, rapidly became critical of the Sandinista revolution, because of its leftwing and even socialist orientation. His mother, and his brothers and sisters, thus supported the right and even the US backed Contra.

Deeply involved in the revolutionary government as director of *Barricada*, Carlos was thus the black sheep of his family. While *La Prensa*, in which his mother, Violeta, and his sister, Christina, were involved, supported the Contra, Carlos directed the newspaper that supported the revolution. And as this division was not only at the level of ideas but led almost daily to numerous casualties - the war unleashed by the Contra in the 80s resulted in about 40 000 casualties - it goes without saying that Carlos's family situation throughout the revolution was extremely painful and taxing.

The surprising and painful electoral defeat of the FSLN in 1990 forced the party to begin a deep reflection on its future direction. Most of the historical leaders of the FSLN argued that the party, which had always functioned in a caudillo and authoritarian manner, something that could be understood in the context of an armed revolution, and then a war initiated by the Contra, had to start functioning in a more democratic way. Daniel Ortega, party director, did not agree and took the debate.

Thus, most of the FSLN historical leaders, for example Sergio Ramírez and Ernesto Cardenal, eventually left the party and decided to create a new party, the Sandinista Renewal Movement (MRS), currently headed by Dora María Téllez.

> On January 7, 2019, four police patrols raided the house of Dora María Téllez. Fortunately, she had taken the precaution to go underground. Like Ernesto Cardenal and Sergio Ramirez, Dora is an ex-historic leader of the Sandinista revolution. It was under her leadership that León, the first city to liberate itself from Somoza in 1979, was liberated.[21]

Carlos Chamorro, closer to the MRS than the FSLN, decided to continue his work as a professional journalist. In 1996, he founded the online magazine *Confidencial*, and shortly afterwards began to host two television programs, *Esta Noche*, broadcast Monday through Friday, and *Esta Semana*, broadcast on Sunday evening. These programs quickly made him one of the most renowned and respected journalists in Nicaragua.

In his reports, Carlos regularly denounced, as any good journalist must do, government shortcomings and misdeeds. When Ortega, who returned to power in 2007, eventually became the object of Chamorro's criticisms and corruption, Ortega often reacted by launching a smear campaign against the messenger.

This is what happened in 2007 when *Esta Semana* reproduced a segment of soundtrack in which one can hear a businessman being offered a bribe of $ 4 million in a case involving a land dispute with peasant cooperatives. The person who offered the bribe: none other than a confidante of Ortega!

---

[21] Wilfredo Miranda Aburto, "Dora María Téllez: Allanar mi casa demuestra "desespere" de la dictadura," (Dora María Téllez : Raiding My House Shows How Desperate the Dictatorship Is) January 8, 2019. Accessed the same day.

In the days that followed, the state television channel accused the businessman, his associates and Chamorro of drug trafficking. The photo of Chamorro appeared on television, and below the photo, the message: "Wanted. Crimes: theft of land, fraud in a cooperative business, attempted bribe and illegal export, falsification of documents".[22]

During the popular uprising of April 2018, Carlos seeks, as *100% Noticias* and the other independent media, to cover the events. And *Confidencial*'s readers are growing rapidly, as well as the audience of *Esta Noche* and *Esta Semana*, while state television and the majority of television channels owned by the Ortega family are losing both audience and credibility.

In mid-October 2018, Mikel Espinoza, editor-in-chief of the government's digital newspaper, *El 19 Digital*, is fed up and leaves office, taking refuge in Costa Rica. For him, the straw that broke the camel's back was the tragic death of an entire family, including two children, in a fire caused by pro-Ortega paramilitary forces. More precisely, in his own words:

> "Hearing the crying of those children when
> they were burning, and the manipulation of the
> news by the Government. (...) I had seen so
> many people die, so many children, so many
> things that I did not agree with."

Mikel is one of about 50 journalists who have been forced to leave Nicaragua. Interviewed by Patricia Martínez in Costa Rica, he claims to have received the order, at the beginning of the April 2018 uprising, not to report the events:

> "All we were asked to report were the statements
> of the National Police and what was said by
> Rosario Murillo.

---

[22] Tina Rosenberg, "The Many Stories of Carlos Fernando Chamorro", *The New York Times Magazine,* March 20, 2009. Accessed August 20, 2018.

> "Espinoza said that as a journalist he felt a 'tremendous blow' when he saw that the policy of the official media was omitting information, reports Martínez. He confessed that there were attacks in which the police and people related to the government participated, and that they as official media had to say that it was the 'right' that was attacking. 'Even though there were photos and witnesses proving that those who attacked were the police, we had to say that the attacks came from the right. (...) The right for Daniel Ortega is everything that opposes the government.' (...) All those who oppose Daniel Ortega are part of the right, the oligarchy: they are considered coup plotters and terrorists."[23]

That in this context, the Ortega government seeks to eliminate the message by repressing the messenger, as Somoza did in the 1970s, is very troubling. Also, and equally disturbing, however, is the attitude of a leftist like Maurice Lemoine who, instead of condemning this repression, finds it normal.

The day I learned that the offices where Carlos Chamorro produced *Confidencial*, *Esta Noche* and *Esta Semana* had been raided by the police, and that the computers and hard drives that were there had been seized, I was in shock. And when, a few days later, I learned that Carlos had to take refuge, with his wife, in Costa Rica, because he was receiving death threats and feared for his life, I felt a great sadness.[24] Similar to the one I experienced in January 1978 when I learned that Somoza had just silenced, by assassination, the

---

[23] Patricia Martínez, "La orden de no informar," (The Order Not to Report) *Confidencial*, October 23, 2018. Accessed October 30, 2018.
[24] Carlos Chamorro, "Periodismo independiente desde el exilio," (Independent Journalism From Exile), *Confidencial*, January 20, 2019, Accessed on the same day.

most renowned Nicaraguan journalist who criticized him, Carlos's father, Pedro Joaquín Chamorro.

Sunday, January 27, 2019, for the first time in 20 years, Nicaraguans could not watch the very popular 8:00 pm television news program *Esta Semana*. Channel 12, which has been broadcasting this program in recent years, has been ordered by the government not to do so.

Should one congratulate Maurice Lemoine for being precise, nuanced, and for not having forgotten the meaning of the word "contextualize" when he calls Carlos Fernando Chamorro "main spokesperson of the right"? Should one congratulate him for not ignoring the part of reality that is not in keeping with his dogmas and beliefs?

OAS Meeting on Nicaragua and the Solis Affair

Welcoming the fact that the Ortega government rejects, in its "aspirations for social justice and respect for democracy, the parody imposed by 'progressives' accrediting the theses of Donald Trump, the OAS, the right-wing Brazilian and Colombian presidents Jair Bolsonaro and Iván Duque, the European Union and mainstream media," Lemoine takes aim at the special meeting convened by the OAS on January 11, 2019 to discuss Nicaragua:

> "On 11 January, following a 'special session' convened by Almagro, the OAS activated the Democratic Charter against Nicaragua. No vote endorsed this decision, no date was announced for a meeting of the General Assembly at which, for this to happen, a favorable vote of 24 of the 34 countries was required - something never achieved against Venezuela. In the latter country, following the script written by the Trump-Almagro-Duque-Bolsonaro axis, the new president of the National Assembly, Juan Guaidó (Voluntad Popular) asked

> on January 11 'the support of the citizens, the
> military and the international community' to
> assume the role of head of state 'usurped' by
> Nicolas Maduro. Already, Almagro has recognized
> him as 'interim president' of Venezuela."

Obviously, Lemoine sees a parallel between the Nicaraguan crisis of April 2018 and the deep crisis into which Venezuela has recently plunged, and which is making the headlines. In both these countries the continental right, supported by the United States, is attempting to hammer in the last nail into the coffin of the Latin American progressive forces. In both of these countries, according to Lemoine, one finds a government aspiring for social justice and respect for democracy and rejecting the "parody imposed by 'progressives' accrediting the theses of Donald Trump, the OAS, the right-wing presidents of Brazil and Colombia Jair Bolsonaro and Iván Duque, the European Union and mainstream media."

As I noted at the very beginning of this book, I will limit myself, in my criticism of Lemoine, to what he says about Nicaragua, a country that I have been visiting annually for many years and of which I have a deeper understanding. Knowing little about Venezuela, except what everyone can learn from reading newspapers, I will refrain from making any judgment about his analysis of this country.

At the end of the article that I am presently commenting, Lemoine reproduces an interview he conducted on January 8, 2019 with Nicaraguan Foreign Minister Denis Moncada Colindres. In this interview, Moncada affirms that Luis Almagro, Secretary General of the OAS, is "only an agent of the United States and the American Empire" and that his only objective is to "follow the orders of the United States, a country that, observing with discontent the fact that President Ortega governs in favor of the vast majority, seeks to destabilize Nicaragua and change the government by illegal means."

On January 11, 2019, at the special session of the OAS on Nicaragua, Moncada delivered a 40-minute speech in which he argued tooth and nail that his country was the victim of a coup attempt, but completely ignored a recent fact that represents a real earthquake for the Ortega-Murillo couple: the surprising and spectacular resignation of one of the closest and most faithful allies of the couple in power, Rafael Solis.

Solis played a key role for the couple for many years. It is he who in 1999 helped Ortega to concoct a pact with the former president, Arnoldo Alemán, which offered three advantages. First, as mentioned above, it allowed both to escape criminal prosecution, Ortega for sexually abusing Zoilamérica, and Alemán for pocketing a substantial portion of international aid following Hurricane Mitch. Secondly, the pact gave Ortega considerable influence over the Supreme Court and the Supreme Electoral Council, something that would eventually serve him well in the future: he could use judges to persecute his political opponents and the Supreme Electoral Council to stay in power by committing with impunity massive electoral fraud. Thirdly, it gave Ortega a very important electoral advantage: it reduced to 35% of the popular vote the percentage needed to win the presidency in the first round (previously it was 45%). Ortega knew, thanks to numerous past polls, that the FSLN could only get about 35% of the popular vote. By concluding a pact with a man like Alemán, whose corruption was so gross and blatant that it had caused a split in the Liberal Party, Ortega not only significantly reduced the percentage needed for the FSLN to win an election, but he also accentuated the conflict already present within the Liberal Party, thus diminishing the chances of this party, his main opponent, to win the elections. Two birds with one stone!

It is still Solis who, in 2005, was best man at the Ortega-Murillo wedding and who, in 2016, developed a strategy so that Ortega could run for the elections, even though doing so was unconstitutional.

On January 8, 2019, the same day that Moncada granted an interview to Lemoine, Solis went to Costa Rica where he wrote a long letter announcing his resignation, both from the Supreme Court of Nicaragua and the FSLN party in which he had been playing a key role since 43 years. The reasons he gave for his astounding move are scathing: Ortega-Murillo's narrative according to which the popular uprising of April 2018 reflects a coup attempt, orchestrated and financed by the Nicaraguan right with financial support from the United States, is unfounded. This couple is responsible for most of the dead, wounded and political prisoners, and the current free fall of the Nicaraguan economy. It is carrying on like an absolute monarchy, controlling all state institutions, including the judiciary and even the Supreme Court of Justice. By clinging to power through sheer repression, by silencing the independent media and by refusing the National Dialogue under the mediation of the Catholic Church supported by the vast majority of Nicaraguans, the Ortega-Murillo couple is sowing the seeds of a possible war civil.[25]

If one can understand, without necessarily excusing, the fact that Denis Moncada carefully avoided in his long speech to the OAS as shocking and earthquake-like an event as the Solis Affair, it is difficult to understand Lemoine's total silence about this event which undermines his main thesis about what happened in Nicaragua.

****

---

[25] Yader Luna, "Rafael Solís: primera fractura en el orteguismo," (Rafael Solis: First Rift in Ortega Regime), *Confidencial*, January 12, 2019. Accessed on the same day.

The taxi driver, who drove me from Hostal Santa Maria to Bufé Laprado in Managua on January 31, 2018, offers another perspective than that of Moncada and Lemoine to interpret the popular uprising that would occur a few months later, in April 2018. Unlike Lemoine, he does not admire the Ortega government's "aspirations for social justice and respect for democracy". And unlike Moncada and Lemoine, he does not see the United States "observing with discontent the fact that President Ortega governs in favor of the vast majority" as the heart of the problem.

> "I fought with the Sandinistas to overthrow Somoza, explained the taxi driver. Why were we fighting? Because Somoza used fraud to win elections. Because he owned a considerable part of the land and many of the large businesses in Nicaragua. Because he controlled the National Guard and basically set himself above all laws. Because he used force to smash all opposition.

> "And what do we have today? The very leader with whom we fought to liberate Nicaragua from the Somoza dictatorship – and it resulted in more than 40,000 deaths – is now doing the same thing as Somoza. He uses massive fraud to win elections. He owns many of the large businesses in Nicaragua, including most of the TV and radio stations, and newspapers. He controls the Supreme Court and the Supreme Electoral Council. He uses force to smash all opposition. If a friend of Daniel Ortega decides that he wants your house, you're in trouble. There is little one can do to prevent that from happening. It is not the rule of law in present day Nicaragua.

> "I did not vote in the recent election. I would be willing to go to war once again to get rid of this dictatorship."

Conclusion: we must reinvent the left

I believe that Maurice Lemoine's analysis of the situation in Nicaragua reflects a form of arrogance and a complex of intellectual superiority. As I mentioned at the beginning of this article, what I find disturbing and even revolting are not the facts and events he reports, but rather the ones he omits. And above all, it is the contempt which he shows regarding the immense suffering of a people whose great majority is today plunged into mourning, suffering, economic insecurity and fear.

In his article Lemoine draws a parallel between what has been happening in Nicaragua since April 2018 and the current crisis in Venezuela. As I have mentioned above several times, I do not know much about the latter country so I will refrain from making any judgment about his analysis of it. However, I sincerely hope that his knowledge of Venezuela and the roots of its crisis goes far beyond that which he has demonstrated in relation to Nicaragua.

As Ángel Sadomando comments in the Chilean edition of *Le Monde Diplomatique* of July 2018, the left, in its analysis of the Nicaraguan situation, must be careful that its ideas and convictions, instead of fostering understanding, do not actually impede it, ideas and convictions becoming like a pair of tinted glasses that allow one to see only certain facts, and not many other, even fundamental ones:

> "Nicaragua's present drama reopens a debate
> about what is acceptable and what is not, about

what arguments explain what is happening and why it is happening. One always filters things according to one's mindset, but it is hard to understand that individuals who consider themselves to be well informed would actually ignore basic facts. Every time there is evidence of fever, such individuals, instead of acknowledging the fever, simply break the thermometer", asserts Ángel Saldomando.

And he continues: "Subordinating facts to a body of dogmatic-religious affirmations, generates an insurmountable contradiction between the owners of truth and the others. And when this kind of subordination gets carried away, this opens the door to all kinds of aberrations. History is plagued by such aberrations, and numerous were those who justified and legitimized them, presenting the version of others as mere lies. Thus, concentration camps, mass repression, and despotic regimes were not acknowledged. (…) That those responsible for the latter were ideologically on one's side sufficed to absolve them."[26]

When I wrote my recent book *Roots of the Crisis: Nicaragua 2018*, there is one source I found that was very moving. Its author, a young Nicaraguan demonstrator, did not dare to give his name, just signing Juanónimo. Today he may be dead, injured, or a refugee in Costa Rica.

As this testimony reflects the essence of what led me to write this review of Maurice Lemoine, I am reproducing it in full below.

---

[26] "Nicaragua : otra vez poder y sangre," (Nicaragua: Power and Blood Once Again), *Le Monde diplomatique*, Chilean edition, July, 2018. Accessed July 25, 2018.

Heartfelt testimony of a protester

"Forget preambles and introductions. Who I am matters little. I'm one of the many who has been wearing a mask. I was born in Nicaragua in the middle of the war and the Revolution of the 80s. From my mother I learned the values of Sandinism and to be committed to social justice. And my father ... I only have a photo of him dressed as a militia; he was carrying me in his arms a few days after I was born.

"I am one of the many who had to put on a mask when the government unmasked itself.

"What drives me today - or rather obliges me - to write these lines is a feeling of rage, of 'encachimbamiento' as we say here - which comes from deep inside, a rage felt by a multitude of Nicaraguans. (…)

"This feeling of rage is like a state of internal fermentation, the fruit of multiple and repeated, setbacks, anger, frustrations and humiliations, all buried in one's subconscious and whose slow maceration ends up suddenly wiping out fear and causing highly flammable vapours. And it is precisely the eruption of this rage that triggered the crisis in which Nicaragua is immersed since April 19.

"But now another rage has started boiling in me and in many of my comrades. We are very upset, even mad, at the reaction of the traditional international left to Nicaragua's present crisis.

"Very upset about this traditional left, with its doubts, its misgivings and its silences that basically make it an accomplice of the bloody repression exerted against a genuine movement of civic insurrection. (…) Because while these high priest leftists are busy debating and glossing in their forums and their think tanks about 'soft coups' , 'color revolutions' and the imperialist theses of Gene Sharp, the thugs of the Ortega-Murillo regime, emboldened and strengthened in their 'revolutionary' holy war, are busy carrying out a systematic manhunt, kidnapping and killing opponents - preferably unarmed, of course - that they portray as 'vandals', 'criminals' and 'terrorists'.

"What marvellous ideological theses these are, capable of transforming what is a legitimate social protest into a mere CIA coup plot! And how useful for Ortega and Murillo, who can defend the businesses they own and justify their numerous misdeeds while presenting themselves as irreproachable revolutionaries being harassed by a horde of young 'right-wing vandals financed by Imperialism' ... youths who were just trying to do exactly what they did 40 years ago during the revolution, remove a dictator! How ironic!

"And what contempt! Could it be that whenever a popular uprising is not framed within an adequate strategic context, does not take place at the right time, and is not decided by them and directed by them, it has no validity? Could it be that struggling against a dictatorship is okay when the latter is right-wing, but not okay when it proclaims itself to be left-wing.

"It must be that we are young, uneducated, short-sighted, with no theoretical basis and no life experience whatsoever. For what we perceive as a democratic struggle against authoritarianism, they view as a large-scale conspiracy against the left, and a strategic battle that the left, which has been losing space, cannot afford to lose. What bad luck that our struggle would happen to be too similar to those coined 'color revolutions' to be approved by the high priests of revolutions!

"Allow me, gentlemen of the traditional left (I say gentlemen, because unfortunately there are virtually no women in this group) to share the following reflections with you.

"For one thing, we know our history. A story marked by the misfortune of having been born in the backyard of an empire with all that that implies, and also because Nicaragua, before it even existed as a country, was the designated place for the construction of an interoceanic canal, a project that occasioned more than one civil war and many invasions of Yankee marines. (...)

"We are not naive. We know that the gringos will always try to interfere and try to abort or recuperate to their advantage all authentically revolutionary processes of social change, however incipient or soft these may seem.

"However, responding to that ever-existing threat by portraying as a coup any spontaneous popular revolt in which the government is massacring its own people, and this in the name of revolutionary principles, is not only immoral and inadmissible, it is also totally counterproductive. For while that happens, the gringos are able to appear as the good guys, the only protectors of democracy and human rights. And this leaves the left with the uncomfortable role of defending causes that are absolutely indefensible.

"In the name of what principles and what ethics can such perverse and cruel punishment of the Nicaraguan people be justified? Because that's really what this is about: the exemplary punishment of protestors -- ungrateful, unruly, and capricious -- who are causing havoc in the farm that the Ortega-Murillo couple so placidly control.

"How can one govern with such hatred? How deranged must one's mind be to order that hospital doors be closed to young people who are bleeding? Or to fire doctors for the simple fact of having attended to injured protesters? Or to deliver poisoned food to students tending roadblocks? Or to pour acid into the faces of protesters? Or to send someone to kill a policeman who did not want to be part of the massacre? Or to give a bonus 2,500 córdobas per month to municipal workers of Managua for them to go hunting with a license to kill and steal? And when all roadblocks and barricades have been removed, to continue persecuting, issuing threats, kidnapping, and torturing.

"Just to mention some absolutely proven and irrefutable facts.

"To confuse this murderous drift and this nepotism of a banana republic with a socialist, Sandinista or minimally leftist project, to defend it, or even to feign neutrality before it, is not only a gross error, it is a shame that history will hardly forgive.

"It is one thing to recognize that today the empire has refined its methods with strategies much more difficult to detect and more in line with the new era of mass communications and social networks.

"However, it is an altogether different thing to mechanically apply such an analysis to a situation of civil protest or to exempt from responsibility a government just for the fact that it self-proclaims itself socialist and revolutionary. In the name of those sacrosanct principles the population of Nicaragua should not have to endure crimes and horrors that not even Somoza committed in such a short period of time.

"This would be nonsense, an insult to intelligence and above all an attitude of profound elitist contempt for the struggle of unarmed Nicaraguans (for how long ...?), who, after facing repeated abuse from their authoritarian government, lost fear and massively took to the streets, thus recovering their memory and their dignity.

"This would be nonsense, in the first place, because the Ortega-Murillo regime is in no way a progressive government, no matter how much it tries, using a sickening pseudo-revolutionary verbiage, to disguise its neoliberalism. The only thing this government has that is left-wing, is the name and letterhead of its party, a party whose progressive agenda has been completely eliminated by Ortega and Murillo, a party that has been turned into an electoral and repressive tool at the service of their political and economic interests.

"What would Sandino say, he who waged a battle against mining companies installed in Nicaragua, were he to discover that the government that today usurps his name has sold most of the subsoil of the country to large extractive multinationals? Not to mention the sale of the concession for the construction of the interoceanic canal to a dubious Chinese company, and arbitrarily seizing land from peasants without even consulting them or at least trying to negotiate with them and obtaining their consent.

> **Information added by Ovide Bastien**
>
> In Sacrificios humanos de la izquierda (Human Sacrifices of the Left),[27] José Luis Rocha notes :
>
> "Under the Ortega regime, mining expanded like never before. According to official figures, available on the website of the Central Bank of Nicaragua, gold exports grew very rapidly: from 99,400 troy ounces and 55.3 million dollars in 2006 to 236,900 troy ounces and 357 million dollars in 2016 (...). Silver exports followed the same rapid growth: from 94,200 to 681,700 troy ounces. Thanks to the adoption of the Nicaraguan Mining Company (ENIMINAS) in 2017, the territory granted to mining went from 12,000 to 26,000 square kilometers."

"What is left-wing about a man capable of concocting numerous schemes in order to perpetuate himself in power, he, his wife and their numerous sons and daughters, each of them in charge of companies, businesses, concessions, TV channels, etc.?

"How can a man like Ortega continue being a reference of the left after it has been more than proven that he sexually abused his stepdaughter Zoilamérica for several years, when she was still a teenager?

---

[27] *Confidencial*, February 14, 2019. Accessed the same day.

"How can a man be considered left-wing after agreeing with the Catholic Church on a medieval law that criminalizes abortion, even if it is therapeutic? (…)

"Dear left-wing intellectuals: instead of continuing to twist reality to make it fit into your obsolete theories, instead of defending the indefensible, try to at least find a hole in your speculations to justify that a handful of very revolted people -- without weapons, without resources, and with no contact whatsoever with the CIA -- have the right to exist, to express themselves and to fight for their rights and their progressive ideals. (…)

"The left is now facing urgent and pressing challenges and this in a new context, one in which there are no clear questions and no clear answers and much fewer absolute certainties or theories. There are things that the left does not manage to understand. But there is something much worse than not understanding: being convinced that one understands and coming up with inappropriate answers. Be it as it may, there are principles, in the meantime, that must be grasped. Without ethics and humanism there is no such thing as a left, concludes Juanónimo." [28]

Ovide Bastien,
Entrelacs,
February 15, 2019

---

[28] "Hay que reinventar la izquierda, que está urgentemente enfrentada a retos nuevos en un contexto nuevo," (We Must Reinvent the Left, which Urgently Faces New Challenges in a New Context), *Nicaragua Investiga*, August 8, 2018. Accessed August 15, 2018.